SHE SANG

FOR THE
MOUNTAINS

THE STORY OF SINGER, SONGWRITER, ACTIVIST *Jean Ritchie*

SHANNON HITCHCOCK & ILLUSTRATIONS BY SOPHIE PAGE

REYCRAFT
BOOKS

In the Cumberland Mountains of Kentucky,
Jean Ritchie heard music everywhere.

In the twinkling stream,
    in the hoot owl's call,

    when the rain played a lullaby
on the farmhouse roof.

The Ritchie family loved to sing.

On sunny spring mornings, Jean's older brothers
and sisters sang in the cornfield.

Jean toted the water.
She always sang along.

On soft summer evenings, Jean nestled on the
porch swing beside her mother.

Dad strummed his dulcimer, and the whole family "sang the moon up"
as the porch swing creaked in time.

OOO-OOO-OOO-OOO!

On crisp autumn evenings,
they sang ghost songs
around the crackling fire.
Jean shivered with fright.

On snowy winter nights,
Jean snuggled in her featherbed
as the wind whistled
through the chimney.

Music was everywhere,
if you knew how to listen.

Jean grew like a sapling,
and life in the Cumberland Mountains
began to change.

Rumbling cars replaced rambling walks.
The roar of radios
replaced the strum of strings.

A heavy feeling hung over the hills.
Jean wished she could turn back time.

Her brothers and sisters left home one by one.
Finally, it was Jean's turn to go.

She took a dulcimer
and a heart full of music,

moved from the quiet
mountains to the noise of
New York City, and became
a music teacher.

Jean taught the songs of the hills
to the children of the city—
songs that had echoed through
the mountains for generations.

Her clear, lilting voice caught the ear of a song collector.

He recorded her ballads for the Library of Congress,
and introduced her to folk singers, who harmonized and protested.

Woody Guthrie

Pete Seeger

Carl Sandburg

Doc Watson

Though Jean was far from home,
she had something to protest, too.

Companies who mined the coal and moved on.
Leaving behind old men with black lung disease,
young men in need of work,
and rusty railroad cars.

PROTECT EARTH

COAL

NO COAL

NOW! SAVE WORKERS

Jean raised her voice and sang for the mountains.

I was born and raised in the mouth of the Hazard Hollow

Coal cars rambled past my door

Now they're standin' in a rusty row all empty

And the L&N

Don't stop here anymore

Jean published her protest songs under the name Than Hall. She believed a man's music would be taken more seriously.

The coal companies started strip mining—
digging and blasting into the mountains.
It poisoned the water.

Again, Jean raised her voice and sang for the mountains.

I come from the mountains, Kentucky's my home

Where the wild deer and black bear so lately did roam

By the cool rushing waterfall the wildflowers dream

And through every green valley, there runs a clear stream

Now there's scenes of destruction on every hand

And only black waters run down through my land

"Black Waters" became a rallying cry.
Protesters linked arms
and stood in front of bulldozers and coal trucks.
They sang for the mountains, just like Jean.

Strip mining gave way to mountaintop removal—
blowing the tops off mountains to mine for coal.

It ripped trees from the forests,
filled valleys with rocks and dirt,
left the mountains desolate, bare, and ugly.

Jean wrote another song—an environmental hymn.
She raised her voice and sang for the mountains.

My Lord, he said unto me,

"Do you like my garden so fair?

You may live in this garden if you'll keep the grasses green.

And I'll return in the cool of the day."

Jean's singing inspired other people to raise their voices, too.
Activists solemnly sang "The Cool of the Day" at their protest rallies.
Jean sang it to throngs of people at the Concert for the Mountains
in New York City.

Jean moved back to Kentucky.
The seasons of her life had passed one by one.

Now she was an old woman.
But some things remained the same.
She kept singing for the mountains
and heard music everywhere.

In the twinkling stream,
in the hoot owl's call,
when the rain played a lullaby on the farmhouse roof.

As Jean's life came to an end,
her family gathered 'round to sing her into heaven.
It was a sad goodbye to Jean, but not to her music.

To this day, Jean's music lives on,
in the hearts of folksingers,
dulcimer players,
and activists,

...who raise their voices and sing for the mountains."

AUTHOR'S NOTE

Jean Ritchie was born to Abigail and Baylis Ritchie on December 8, 1922, in Viper, Kentucky. She was the youngest of fourteen children, one of whom died from diphtheria. Jean's mother tended the house, while her dad was a jack-of-all-trades. He farmed, taught school, sold eyeglasses, and even printed a newspaper.

The Ritchie family lived primitively by today's standards. Walled in by the Cumberland Mountains, they entertained themselves with ballads that had been handed down for generations.

Singing was an everyday occurrence in the Ritchie family. Jean's mom sang while she cooked, cleaned, and churned butter. The children sang in the cornfield, and as they went about their chores. Most nights found the family singing after supper, on the front porch in summer, or by the fireplace in winter.

Jean graduated from the University of Kentucky with a degree in social work. She moved to New York City to work at the Henry Street Settlement House. There she taught her family's songs to the children and was introduced to musicologist Alan Lomax. Mr. Lomax recorded Jean's songs for the Library of Congress Folksong Archives.

In 1952, Jean won a Fulbright scholarship. She used it to travel through the British Isles, tracing the sources of her family's songs.

Over the years, Jean sang at Carnegie Hall, at London's Royal Albert Hall, and many times at the Newport Folk Festival in Rhode Island. She played with some of the most famous names in folk music, including Woody Guthrie, Doc Watson, and Pete Seeger.

Though Jean performed with Mr. Seeger, she said of him, "Pete Seeger never got over the notion that I only sang ballads." Jean also had trouble with Bob Dylan. He used one of her family's tunes on his song, "Masters of War." Mr. Dylan settled out of court, and though he took his name off as composer, he never acknowledged where the music came from.

In addition to performing centuries-old ballads, Jean wrote songs of her own. The most famous ones, "The L&N Don't Stop Here Anymore," "Black Waters," and "The Cool of the Day," lament how coal mining is destroying the landscapes of Appalachia.

Jean also recorded several albums and wrote numerous books, including her autobiography, *Jean Ritchie, Singing Family of the Cumberlands*, which was illustrated by Maurice Sendak.

In 2002, Jean was awarded a National Heritage Fellowship from the National Endowment for the Arts. She is credited with bringing hundreds of old songs from her native Kentucky to a wide audience. Joan Baez called her the "Mother of Folk."

Jean died on June 1, 2015. She was ninety-two years old.